j973
Duvall
   Tuscarora

E20519

DATE DUE

DEC 3 1996			
OCT 1 8 2002			

A New True Book

THE TUSCARORA

By Jill D. Duvall

CP CHILDRENS PRESS ®

CHICAGO

Tuscaroras are known for
their colorful beadwork.

PHOTO CREDITS

© Reinhard Brucker—21; © Northern Illinois
University Museum, 8 (top left & bottom left); © Field
Museum, Chicago, 8 (right); © Milwaukee Public
Museum, 11

© Gina Henry—30

Historical Pictures Service—36 (left)

Photo by courtesy of the National Gallery of
Art—29 (right)

National Museum of American Art, Washington, D.C./
Art Resource, NY—27

New York State Department of Economic
Development—19

North Wind Picture Archives—6, 9, 13, 14, 17

© Ron Roels—32, 33, 34, 36 (right)

© Smithsonian Institution—29 (left—neg #39B)

Photograph Courtesy of Smithsonian Institution
National Museum of the American Indian—Cover
Inset (neg #4233), 2 (neg #4233)

SuperStock International, Inc.—31

UPI/Bettmann—39

© 1990 Steve Wall—45

© Joanne Weinholtz—Cover, 4 (2 photos), 23, 25, 26
(2 photos), 40 (2 photos), 41, 42 (2 photos), 43, 44
(3 photos)

Cover—Joanne Rickard-Weinholtz, Tuscarora Nation,
    Turtle Clan

Cover Inset—Black velvet bag with beadwork

Library of Congress Cataloging-in-Publication Data

Duvall, Jill D.
    The Tuscarora / by Jill D. Duvall.
        p.   cm. — (A New true book)
    Includes index.
    Summary: Describes the history, changing fortunes,
and way of life of the Tuscarora.
    ISBN 0-516-01128-6
    1. Tuscarora Indians—Juvenile literature.
[1. Tuscarora Indians. 2. Indians of North
America.] I. Title.
E99.T9D97   1991   91-3037
973'.04975—dc20   CIP
                                      AC

TABLE OF CONTENTS

Jolene Sue Gansworth models a traditional Tuscarora outfit. The turtle
on the back of her shirt shows that she is a member of the Turtle Clan.

A BROKEN VINE

A very old story is still
told to Tuscarora children.
It tells of the beginnings
of their nation.

Long ago, the "original
people" were moving to
new hunting grounds. In
their path was a dangerous
river. The people found a
grapevine stretched across
the river. By holding on to
the vine, they could get
safely to the other side.

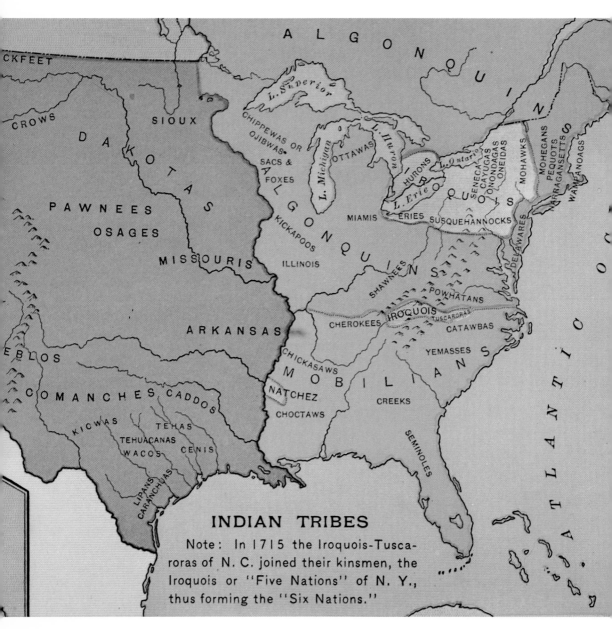

INDIAN TRIBES

Note: In 1715 the Iroquois-Tuscaroras of N. C. joined their kinsmen, the Iroquois or "Five Nations" of N. Y., thus forming the "Six Nations."

The Tuscarora settled in North Carolina. The Mohawk, Seneca, Cayuga, Oneida, and Onondaga settled in what is now New York State.

However, when most of
them had crossed, the
vine broke! Those who had
crossed the river moved
on. The others were left
behind.

The group that crossed
the dangerous river was
the Tuscarora. The others
were the Mohawk, Seneca,
Oneida, Onondaga, and
Cayuga nations. They
became the Five Nations
of the Iroquois Confederacy.

The Iroquois used natural materials like wood and reeds to make bowls, tools, and baskets.

This story may explain why the Tuscarora—who lived hundreds of miles from the Oneida, Cayuga, Onondaga, Seneca, and Mohawk nations— spoke an Iroquoian language.

LIFE IN NORTH CAROLINA

The Tuscarora called themselves *Skarooren*, meaning "people of the Indian hemp." When only Native Americans lived in North America, Tuscarora villages spread from the

The houses in Tuscarora villages were made by covering a frame of wooden poles with sheets of tree bark.

Appalachian Mountains to the Atlantic Ocean. They were the largest and strongest group in the area.

Many kinds of vegetables grew in the rich soil of their large villages. Fruits and nuts grew in the forests. Nearby rivers and streams were filled with delicious fish.

The Tuscarora made woven baskets to hold fruits and nuts gathered from the forest.

Spring was a beautiful time for the Tuscarora. Their land was filled with flowering trees and newborn animals. When the short winters arrived, whole villages moved to their hunting grounds in the woods.

11

Until the early 1700s, life was mostly good for the Tuscarora. There were many thousands of other Native Americans in the area. Sometimes they had disagreements. These were settled quickly by small bands of warriors. But even in wartime, women and children were seldom harmed.

The first European settlers who came to
North Carolina were friends with the Tuscarora.

THE EUROPEAN SETTLERS

At first, the Tuscarora
were friends with the
Europeans. But once a
great many non-Indian
settlers had come to the
land of the Tuscarora, this

13

The settlers cut down the forests to build
log houses and to clear fields for crops.

changed. Soon the Swiss,
German, and English
settlers all wanted to
expand their own farms.
So, they just took over
more Tuscarora land.

At first the North Carolina Indians were not worried. There seemed to be enough land for everyone to use. But that changed, too.

No one is quite sure what spark started the final trouble. Some say certain Europeans came to the Tuscarora with warnings that the latest settlers wanted all their land. Others said the

Tuscarora were angry because many members of their nation were being sold into slavery. Many Tuscarora were taken to work on plantations far away.

One day, a band of Tuscarora warriors raided a settlement that the European colonists had established on their land. Over 200 people were killed.

Thousands of Tuscarora died fighting the settlers. Many more died from the diseases they caught from the settlers.

North Carolinians asked neighboring colonies to send soldiers to fight the Tuscarora. South Carolina sent Colonel John Barnwell. With him came about 500 Yamasee fighters. The Tuscarora and the Yamasee had been enemies for a long time.

Barnwell's army killed many Tuscarora. After the fighting stopped, the two sides signed a peace agreement. But when Barnwell was not paid by the colonists, he became angry. He broke the peace agreement. Many more Tuscarora were killed. Others were sold into slavery. Barnwell said that this was his way of

Tuscarora wearing Native American
clothes at the Tuscarora Museum

getting payment for his
part in defeating the
Tuscarora.

Other settlers fought
with the Tuscarora, too. By
1713, the Tuscarora
leaders were divided. Their
way of life was threatened. **19**

Most of their men had already been killed. Unless something was done, they feared that every member of their nation would be killed.

One group of Tuscarora asked the Iroquois Confederacy for help. The Five Nations held a council. An Oneida chief spoke for the Tuscarora. All the chiefs agreed to adopt the entire Tuscarora nation.

A NEW HOMELAND

Most of the Tuscarora started moving north right away. It took years for them to reach their new home.

Since the Oneida had asked the Confederacy to

Several families lived in each Iroquois longhouse. They slept on furs piled on the platforms along the sides.

adopt the Tuscarora, they were settled on land between the territories of the Oneida and Onondaga. In 1722, when the adoption was complete, the Tuscarora became the sixth nation of the Iroquois Confederacy.

After the American Revolution, most Iroquois sold their territory to the state of New York. This left the Tuscarora without a homeland again.

The council house on the Tuscarora reservation

After many years and through a number of agreements, a reservation for the Tuscarora was pieced together in 1842, with the help of the Seneca. Finally, the Tuscarora had a permanent home, though it is not very large.

LIFE TODAY

The Tuscarora reservation is nine miles from Niagara Falls, New York. It is still governed in the traditional way. Clan mothers still select men to represent the voice of the people.

The reservation land, 5,700 acres of it, is held in trust by the whole Tuscarora nation. All the businesses on the

Three generations of one family. Tuscarora
families like to stay together.

reservation are owned by
Tuscarora or their Native
American guests from other
nations. Family groups have
rights to use reservation
land. These rights are
passed on through the
mother's clan.

25

Joanne Rickard-Weinholtz is a
teacher at the Tuscarora school (left).
She is wearing a traditional dress
with a beaded collar made by her mother.

In other ways, the
Tuscarora live like their
non-Indian neighbors. The
men and women have jobs
in nearby cities. The
children go to school off
the reservation after the
sixth grade.

COURAGEOUS TUSCARORA

Nicholas Cusick

A number of Tuscarora are remembered in U.S. history. Nicholas Cusick helped General George Washington. He also befriended the Marquis de Lafayette, Washington's

27

friend, during the American Revolution.

Cusick's loyalty and sharpshooting skill made him a courageous fighter during the War of 1812.

Cornelius C. Cusick was Nicholas's grandson. During the American Civil War, Cornelius was a captain. He was so brave that Native Americans living west of the Mississippi began using the expression "brave as a Tuscarora."

J. N. B. Hewitt (left). The famous artist
George Catlin painted this picture (above)
of Tuscarora men and a woman.

David Cusick recorded
some of the earliest
accounts of Tuscarora life.

J. N. B. Hewitt was a
Tuscarora scholar. His
works are among the
finest accounts of Native
Americans ever written.

Lois Henry visits a statue of her father, Clinton Rickard, at Niagara Falls.

CHIEF CLINTON RICKARD

Chief Clinton Rickard was the great-nephew of Nicholas Cusick. He was responsible for one of the proudest events in Native American history.

On its way from Lake Erie to Lake Ontario,
the Niagara River drops over Niagara Falls.

Every year, on the third
Saturday of July, Border
Crossing Day is celebrated
by the Iroquois and other
Indians. One year the crowd
gathers on the Canadian
side of Niagara Falls. The
next year, the parade begins
on the United States side.
Everybody then crosses

Crossing the bridge at Niagara Falls on Border Crossing Day

the bridge between the two countries.

The border crossing signifies that the lands of the Iroquois Confederacy still belong to one nation. They are not separated by the Canadian-U.S. border.

Hundreds of people celebrate all day long. There are baseball and lacrosse games, speeches, songs, and dancing. Corn

A Tuscarora carrying the Canadian flag leads the way across the border.

soup and corn bread are special treats.

The man responsible for this celebration was Clinton Rickard. He was born at Tuscarora in 1882. Chief Rickard worked

Chief Clinton Rickard (right) in 1965

hard for Native American rights. He founded the Indian Defense League, which is still at work.

Clinton Rickard proved that President George Washington and the U.S. Congress had guaranteed that the Native Americans would not be separated from each other by the Canadian-U.S. border.

This promise was made in the Jay Treaty of 1794. President Washington was

Border Crossing Day ceremonies (right). Tuscarora and other Iroquois nations remember the signing of the Jay Treaty under George Washington (left).

very grateful for help from the Tuscarora. He wanted to be sure that they always had a homeland. The Jay Treaty also declared that the Native Americans had the right to rule their own nations.

In 1924, the U.S. Congress passed a new

36

immigration law. The law claimed that Native Americans were no longer able to go freely back and forth between Canada and the United States. It was Clinton Rickard who reminded the U.S. government of the 1794 Jay Treaty.

Although Border Crossing Day is fun, it is also a serious and important reminder of rights granted to Native Americans living on both sides of the border.

RESERVATION LIFE

Only about 1,000 Tuscaroras live on the reservation near Niagara. Many Tuscarora live off the reservation.

In 1957, the New York State Power Authority decided it needed to put a reservoir in the Niagara area. The Tuscarora council resisted this plan. Chiefs Elton Greene and Harry Patterson fought the plan all the way to the U.S. Supreme Court. The case was lost, but the spirit that resisted the taking of Native American land is still alive in the Tuscarora nation.

Chief Elton Greene points to a map of Tuscarora land that was taken by the New York State Power Authority.

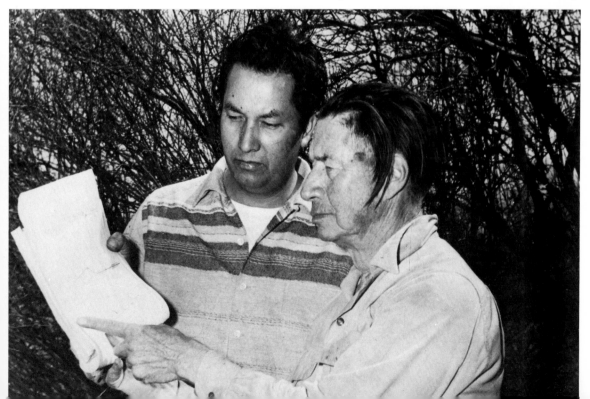

Braiding of the Tuscarora traditional white corn—ears of corn are husked and then braided together.
The husks are saved to make corn-husk dolls.

The Tuscarora are among the most respected of the Native American peoples. Each new generation is taught the

traditions of their

ancestors. There are many religions among the Tuscarora today. They believe all people should have freedom of religion.

Gina Henry is a member of the Tuscarora Bear Clan.

Tyler Rickard (left) displays a traditional outfit and headpiece.
Jolene Sue Gansworth (right) models her cheerleader costume.

Today, Tuscarora
children are being taught
the history of the Iroquois
Confederacy. The
Tuscarora language is also
being taught.

Life has been difficult
for Native Americans since
Europeans took their lands.
But the nations of the
Iroquois Confederacy are
working to preserve their
homelands and traditions.

Beth Rickard,
aged three, checks
the corn crop.

Young Tuscarora Randy Greene (right, in lacrosse uniform), Kehala Greene (below), and Alexandra Weinholtz (bottom right) will live in a modern world that preserves the old traditions

44

Chief Edison
Mount Pleasant
and his wife.
Mrs. Mount Pleasant
is Clan Mother for
the Wolf Clan.

The Tuscarora are sure
the people of the
Confederacy will be fully
reunited one day. They will
no longer be separated by
the rushing river.

WORDS YOU SHOULD KNOW

account (uh • KOWNT) — a story or a report

adopt (uh • DAHPT) — to take in; to make part of a family or other group

ancestor (AN • sess • ter) — a grandparent or forebear earlier in history

colonies (KAHL • uh • neez) — settlements of people who came from another country

confederacy (kun • FED • er • uh • see) — a union of nations, states, or people joined together for some purpose

council (KOWN • sil) — a meeting held to discuss problems and to decide a course of action

disagreement (dis • uh • GREE • mint) — an argument; a dispute

generation (jen • er • RAY • shun) — all the individuals born at about the same time; parents are one generation and children are the next

guaranteed (gair • en • TEED) — made sure of; promised

immigration (im • ih • GRAY • shun) — the coming in of people from other countries

Indian hemp (IN • dee • yen HEMP) — a plant with tough bark and milky white juice

Iroquoian (eer • ih • KWOI • yun) — one of a group of related languages spoken by Indian nations of the eastern woodlands of North America

permanent (PER • muh • nent) — lasting a long time; lasting forever

reminder (ree • MYN • der) — something that helps one to remember something else

reservation (reh • zer • VAY • shun) — a piece of land set aside by the government as a home for Indians

reservoir (REH • zehr • vwahr) — an artificial lake that holds water for drinking or to make electric power

revolution (reh • vih • LOO • shun) — the overthrow of a government

settlers (SET • lerz) — people who come to a new country and establish farms or other homes there

signifies (SIG • nih • fyze) — stands for; represents

survive (ser • VYVE) — to last; to remain alive after great danger or trouble

territory (TAIR • ih • tor • ee) — an area of land that a group of people regard as their own

traditional (truh • DISH • un • il) — following old customs and beliefs

warrior (WAR • ee • er) — a fighter; a soldier

INDEX

About the Author

Jill Duvall is a political scientist who received an M.A. from Georgetown University in 1976. Since then, her research and writing have included a variety of national and international issues. Among these are world hunger, alternative energy, human rights, cross-cultural and interracial relationships. One of her current endeavors is a study of ancient goddess cultures. Ms. Duvall proudly serves as a member of the Board of Managers of the Glenn Mills Schools, a facility that is revolutionizing methods for rehabilitating male juvenile delinquents.